PERFECTION LEARNING®

# Can You See the Wind?

Molly Blaisdell

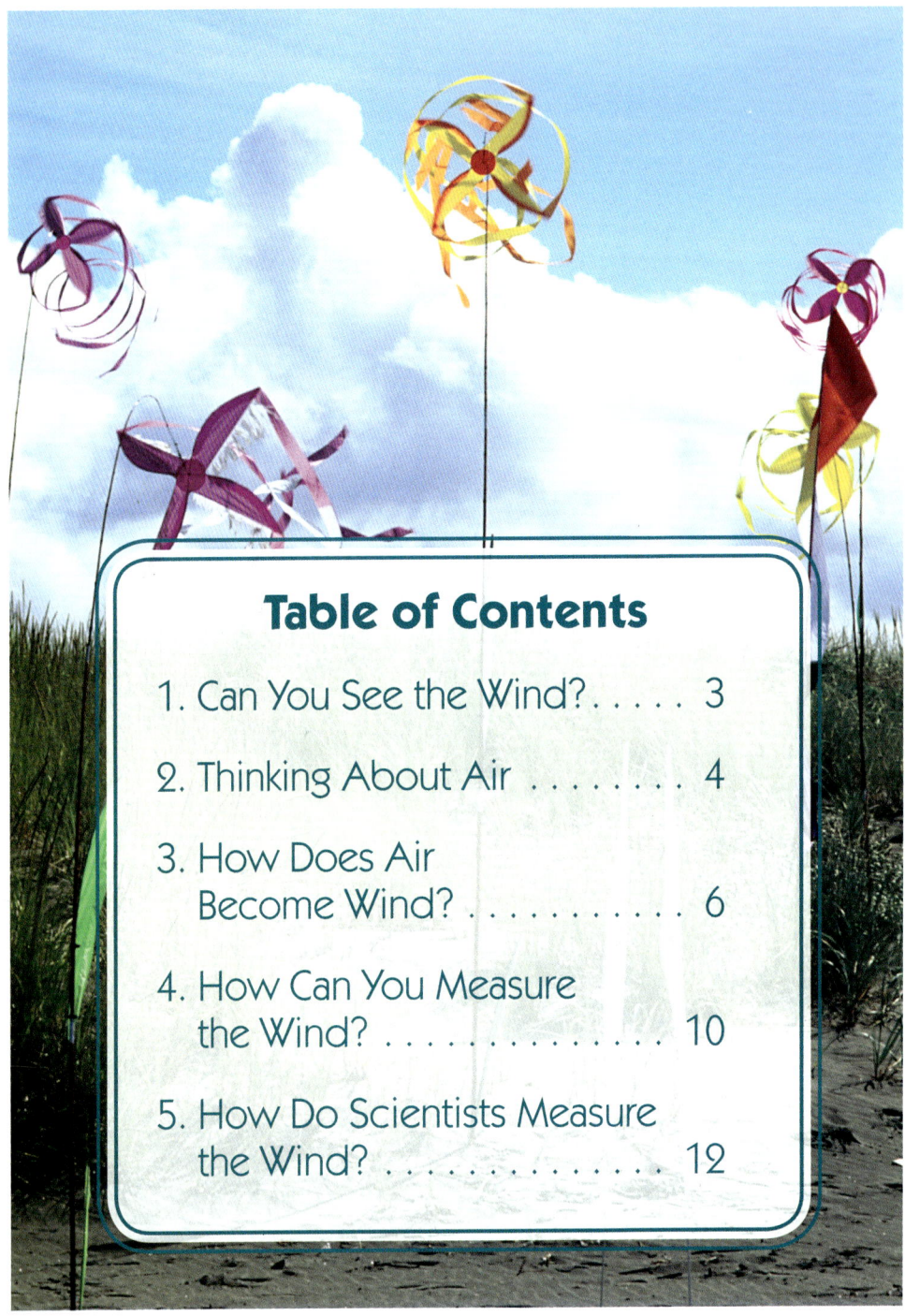

## Table of Contents

1. Can You See the Wind?..... 3

2. Thinking About Air ....... 4

3. How Does Air
   Become Wind? .......... 6

4. How Can You Measure
   the Wind? ............. 10

5. How Do Scientists Measure
   the Wind? ............. 12

CHAPTER 1

# Can You See the Wind?

Have you seen leaves move? Have you felt cool air against your cheek? Have you flown a kite? If you have, you know about the wind. You know that wind cannot be seen. It is invisible.

CHAPTER 2

# Thinking About Air

To understand wind, we must start with air. Air does not have an exact shape and size like a solid. It does not have an exact size like a liquid.

Ice is a solid.

If you pour air into a bottle, it takes on the shape and size of the bottle.

Air is a gas. Air does have something in common with solids and liquids. It has weight.

CHAPTER 3

# How Does Air Become Wind?

Air surrounds the Earth. It is called the *atmosphere*. Our Earth is spinning. Air spins too.

Sun

Warm air rises.

The sun heats the air. Air becomes lighter when it is warm. Warm air rises.

Winds form.

Cool air sinks.

Air becomes heavier when it is cool. Cool air sinks. Air is always moving. Moving air is called *wind*.

CHAPTER 4

# How Can You Measure the Wind?

We can measure the wind by observing it. When the wind is calm, smoke goes straight up. When there is a light breeze, leaves rustle.

When there is a strong breeze, tree branches move. A powerful wind is called a *gale*. Whole trees move in a gale.

CHAPTER 5

# How Do Scientists Measure the Wind?

Scientists measure the wind with instruments. A wind sock is a cone-shaped bag with an opening at both ends. Wind socks show the direction of the wind.

A wind vane also shows the direction of the wind.

An anemometer shows wind speed. Three or four cups are attached to a central stick. Wind blows. The cups spin. A dial on the anemometer shows the wind speed.

Scientists study wind at weather stations all over the world. Measuring wind helps scientists forecast the weather.

# Glossary

Anemometer

Atmosphere

Gale

Weather station

Wind sock

Wind vane

**Discovering Science**

Leveled content-area science books in Earth/Space Science, Life Science, Math in Science, Physical Science, Science and Technology, and Science as Inquiry for emergent, early, and fluent readers

# Can You See the Wind?
### Written by Molly Blaisdell

Text © 2009, 2006 by Perfection Learning® Corporation

All rights reserved. No part of this book may be reproduced, stored in a retrieval system, or transmitted in any form or by any means, electronic, mechanical, photocopying, recording, or otherwise, without prior permission of the publisher.
Printed in the United States of America.

For information, contact
**Perfection Learning® Corporation**
1000 North Second Avenue, P.O. Box 500
Logan, Iowa 51546-0500.
Phone: 1-800-831-4190
Fax: 1-800-543-2745

perfectionlearning.com

PB ISBN-13: 978-0-7891-6720-0   ISBN-10: 0-7891-6720-4
RLB ISBN-13: 9780-7569-8412-0   ISBN-10: 0-7569-8412-2

2  3  4  5  6  7   PP  14  13  12  11  10  09
29857

Book Design: Emily J. Greazel

Image credits:

©INGRAM Publishing Royalty-Free: front cover; ©Andreas Steinbach/iStock International Inc.: back cover; Photos.com: pp. 1, 2, 8–9; NASA: pp. 6–7; BananaStock Royalty Free: p. 3; ©Jin Young Lee/iStock International Inc.: p. 4; ©Betsy Dupuis/iStock International Inc.: p. 5; ©Royalty-Free/Corbis: pp. 10, 11; ©Eddy Lund/iStock International Inc.: p. 12; ©David Phillips/iStock International Inc.: p. 13 (top); ImageSource Royalty-Free: p. 13 (bottom); ©Martin B. Withers; Frank Lane Picture Agency/Corbis: pp. 14–15, 16; ©Associated Press: p. 15